Learner Services

Please return
on or before
the last date
stamped below

CITY COLLEGE
NORWICH

Ma
Ch
A G

D1333901

238   346

of related interest

The Self-Help Guide for Special Kids and their Parents
Joan Matthews and James Williams
ISBN-13: 978 1 85302 914 1   ISBN-10: 1 85302 914 9

Small Steps Forward
Using Games and Activities to Help Your Pre-School Child
with Special Needs
Sarah Newman
ISBN-13: 978 1 85302 643 0   ISBN-10: 1 85302 643 3

Music Therapy with Children
David Aldridge
ISBN-13: 978 1 85302 757 4   ISBN-10: 1 85302 757 X

Music Therapy: Intimate Notes
Mercédès Pavlicevic
ISBN-13: 978 1 85302 692 8   ISBN-10: 1 85302 692 1

Filling a Need While Making Some Noise
A Music Therapist's Guide to Pediatrics
Kathy Irvine Lorenzato
Foreword by Kay Roskam
ISBN-13: 978 1 84310 819 1   ISBN-10: 1 84310 819 4

Interactive Music Therapy – A Positive Approach
Music Therapy at a Child Development Centre
Amelia Oldfield
Foreword by Dr Fatima Janjua
ISBN-13: 978 1 84310 309 7   ISBN-10: 1 84310 309 5

Music Therapy in Children's Hospices
Jessie's Fund in Action
Edited by Mercédès Pavlicevic
Foreword by Victoria Wood
ISBN-13: 978 1 84310 254 0   ISBN-10: 1 84310 254 4

Music Therapy, Sensory Integration and the Autistic Child
Dorita S. Berger
Foreword by Donna Williams
ISBN-13: 978 1 84310 700 2   ISBN-10: 1 84310 700 7

Autism, Play and Social Interaction
Lone Gammeltoft and Marianne Sollok Nordenhof
Translated by Erik van Acker
ISBN-13: 978 1 84310 520 6   ISBN-10: 1 84310 520 9

Making Music with the Young Child with Special Needs

A Guide for Parents
Revised Edition

Elaine Streeter

Jessica Kingsley Publishers
London and Philadelphia

First published and distributed in the United Kingdom
by Music Therapy Publications (ISBN 0 9507145 0 X) 1980

New edition published in 1993
by Jessica Kingsley Publishers
116 Pentonville Road
London N1 9JB, UK
and
400 Market Street, Suite 400
Philadelphia, PA 19106, USA

www.jkp.com

Copyright © Elaine Streeter 1993
Photographs by Prue Bramwell-Davis
Cover photo © Prue Bramwell-Davis

Printed digitally since 2007

Library of Congress Cataloging in Publication Data
A CIP catalog record for this book is available from the Library of Congress

British Library Cataloguing in Publication Data
Streeter, Elaine
Making Music with the Young Child with
Special Needs: Guide for Parents
I. Title
784.19
ISBN-10: 1 85302 960 2

ISBN-10: 1 85302 960 2
ISBN-13: 978 1 85302 960 8

Contents

Acknowledgements

Thanks to:
Jemima, Claire, David, Kelly, Emma, and Paddy.
All the staff at the Children's Day Nursery and at the
Child Development Centre, Charing Cross Hospital.
The parents for their co-operation.

With special thanks to the late Dr Hugh Jolly
who supported and encouraged my work with
young children at the Child Development Centre,
Charing Cross Hospital, London.

A note on language

'She' has been used throughout this book, but 'she' embraces 'he'.

Introduction

Parents know that music is something which their children enjoy. They also sense that it may be an important way of helping a child forward. Over the last twenty years since this book was first published, research into music therapy has shown that early intervention through music can help many young children communicate and start to explore their potential for learning; so making the most of your child's interest in music, as early as possible, is a really useful way of trying to help them.

You probably don't play an instrument or remember how to read music. That doesn't matter. This book has been written for parents and carers who do not necessarily have those skills, so you won't need a piano, a guitar or a violin, and there won't be any confusing crotchets or quavers to have to worry about. You will be introduced to simple musical activities that anyone can try out at home with the help of a few small percussion instruments.

We are all musical people, otherwise we would never buy CDs or tune our radios to particular stations, but many of us doubt whether we are musical at all. We may have learned somewhere along the line that we are 'no good' at music. However, research now shows that parents tune in to the timing of their baby's sounds, with exquisite accuracy, millions of times over without even realising it. So you have been responding musically with your voice, your smile, your touch and your gaze ever since day one. Some people may be more musical than others, and find it easier to play instruments, but gaining confidence in your ability to enjoy making sounds is all that is really needed to get started. This book will help you try out ideas and show you what to do.

So why actually make up music with your child? Why not simply put on a tape? Before they can play with one another, children need to be played with and we now know that music making provides just the right sort of playful relationship through which young children can begin to develop. You can adapt the way you play to meet the pace and timing of your child's own sounds and this is vitally important in the give and take of communication. A tape cannot wait and listen for a child's individual responses, nor can it notice when she looks away or loses concentration. Sitting down on the floor and sharing a few small instruments, such as a drum or chime bar, offers the opportunity for creative play in a language your child is likely, already, to understand – music.

So how come young children already understand music; surely they have to be taught it at school? Sound is one of the first sensory experiences a baby is exposed to, months before they are even born. Inside our mothers we are able to hear a whole variety of sounds, including our mother's heartbeat, the up and down of her voice as well as the muffled background of what she may be listening to on the radio or TV. Babies are not able to make much sense of this but they do experience it and as soon as they are born they begin to use sounds themselves which directly attract our attention. Research has shown that in their first few days babies take in the pitch, rhythm and tone quality of our voices. Then they try to communicate back. Of course pitch, tone and rhythm are the primary building blocks of music and this is perhaps why music is so easy for children to respond to and enjoy. They have been trying to respond to sounds right from the start. All of this can be thought of as making music.

So playing together with sounds will not be time wasted during the pre-school years, for you will be offering something important; the opportunity for interaction at a level and pace your child is likely to feel comfortable with. Parents some-. times spend months, and even years, searching for the right kind of specialist help for their children. In the meantime, by making music on a regular basis, you can be helping your child along the way. Music is an excellent medium through which they can develop and practise communication skills, at whatever level is possible for them. Throughout this book you will be given clear examples of what to try out and shown how musical activities, that you yourself will be able to play, can encourage spontaneity and concentration on the part of your child.

Language develops through meaningful relationships and this is probably the area that concerns you most. Whether or not a child eventually learns to speak depends on many factors. What we do know is that music brings people together in a shared experience, even when they have their back turned or their eyes closed. So your attempts at playing and singing with your child will almost always be heard, or felt, whether or not they are responded to. Some of our earliest memories are often associated with sound: a birthday cake and the singing which accompanied it, sitting on someone's lap being sung to, or even earlier in the warmth of one's parent's arms. These experiences contain far more than the notes which were sung or played, for they hold within them the beginnings of an awareness of love and containment, of belonging and relating. Making up music and sharing it together can engage a child in meaningful communication. Even though you may not use words, you will be letting your child know that you are sharing her world.

By showing you how to start playing simple musical instruments with your child at home and giving you the confidence to enjoy making music yourself, I hope you will find this book useful.

Elaine Streeter

Part 1

How Can Music Help?

How Can Music Help?

Making music can help your child in a number of ways.

Language Development

Whether or not your child can speak, making music can stimulate pre-speech vocal sounds which explore a range of consonants, vowels, pitches and timing. Language isn't all about words, it is also about enjoying communicating. By helping your child explore her voice freely, and playing with the sounds she can create, you will be doing something vitally important: helping her enjoy exploring her voice.

Because she is interested in the sound of music your child will automatically be listening more carefully and this is one of the first steps towards 'conversation'.

Children normally understand a lot more language than they can use at first. If their hearing is OK they will have been listening to all the talking going on around them for a long time before they use speech themselves. They spend this time trying to imitate the sounds they hear, even though they may not understand completely what is meant. Then they attempt various versions of words themselves, starting with very simple sounds like 'mama' and 'dada'. They go on imitating and inventing for some time and even keep some of their own favourite words, for example 'biscetti' instead of 'spaghetti'. Notice that the rhythm is exactly the same in the two 'words' but the consonants and vowels aren't quite accurate.

So recognising and imitating rhythm is one of the ways in which children develop language. Of course rhythm is part of music too, so when your child is involved in music making she is also undertaking a form of language learning – because music stimulates rhythmic sound imitation. Waiting, pausing and listening for the child's vocal response is going to be very important, as well as responding to the little sounds she does make, however fleeting they may be. Perhaps it may take a long time before any sounds are made. But as her enjoyment of music increases it is more likely that your child will begin to express herself, spontaneously, through using her voice. Music does not require words. You can sing along with it, without words, and it still makes sense.

A child with special needs may have difficulty in concentration and this will affect her listening ability. Although hearing may be good, some children may not be able to make much sense of what they are hearing. By playing simple musical games together you will be helping to focus your child's listening ability and at the same time giving her the experience of 'conversation'. You won't be using words, you will be using a language she already understands – music. Having musical conversations can help your child to understand what real language is all about; she may not understand why one person stops talking and someone else starts; she may not realise that they are listening to one another. So, sharing a musical phrase and answering a musical phrase are two very simple conversational games that can help.

[A note about hearing: If at any time you are concerned that your child may not be able to hear properly, seek the advice of your doctor or health visitor. Hearing difficulties often result in slow language development, so it is important that hearing is thoroughly tested.]

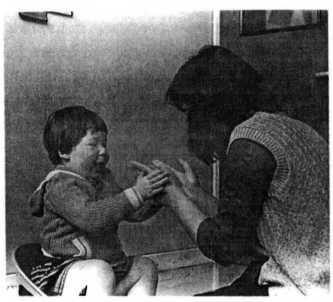

Play

As you probably know, play is an important part of any child's early development. Through play children develop a wide range of skills; learning about shape, size, colour, sensation, how to hold and manipulate objects and how to share things with others. Children quickly want to establish which toy or object 'belongs' to them. 'Mine!' is an exclamation often used. All of this play exploration helps a young child discover the differences between objects and how to use them. At the same time they learn about sharing toys and relating to others.

Accessing play is sometimes not so easy for young children with special needs; even if they are surrounded by toys a whole variety of coordination difficulties may stand in their path. Other children will want to include them in their games, but they may not notice what the child with special needs is trying to do because their own games may be happening very quickly. Most of the skills children develop through play will automatically be part of your music session so by offering music you will be helping your child gain access to play. By working with her at her own pace, however uncoordinated or fleeting that may be, you will be offering her the possibility of gaining confidence in what she can do and in this way you will be helping your child make better use of play with other children.

It may be particularly difficult for a child to start playing with toys and books if she does not easily explore objects. Playing simple musical instruments can help a child understand that using objects can make something happen. If the child can enjoy making music with simple instruments, she may be able to learn more quickly that holding on to something can lead to using it. Because music is an immediate experience, very little time is lost between holding and doing, so you may be able to sustain her attention long enough for her to learn that it is worth holding on to things. Later on, when playing is easier, music can help the child to explore imaginatively. Children love to listen to stories with music; their imagination is stimulated by the different musical ideas in nursery rhymes, for example, and this can help them eventually to develop imaginary games with cars, dolls and animals.

Physical Development

For children with physical disabilities, musical activity can help to define movement sequences. Because the rhythm in music invites movement, your child is likely to be interested in trying to move with the music. You can make the most of this motivation by creating a musical game of crawling, walking or even stretching out. Musical rhythm is not merely a diversion. It will actually help your child to coordinate muscle patterns. Coordination of movement is essential for crawling, walking and running, so even if your child is not ready for any of these movements, giving her the opportunity to play rhythmic music is going to give her the chance to attempt physical coordination. Wanting to move accurately can help the child achieve better coordination and music makes children want to move. Timing is very important. Rather than expecting the child to play at your pace, time your own music to fit in with hers.

Relationships

Some children with special needs find it particularly difficult to relate to others. They may not yet have acquired the kind of social skills necessary to make relationships work. We know from research that when children are deprived of opportunities to relate to others they often become withdrawn. Certain syndromes, like autism, seem to create those circumstances for a child, even though everyone around them is trying their very utmost to make contact with them. It can be desperately hard for parents to find a way of communicating with a child who gives them so little to go on. Music is not the complete answer but it can provide a time of togetherness when your child can be a little easier to get on with because of her interest in music. Music is a shared experience and one which offers hope to children who are isolated and remote. It can be experienced on many different levels, but unless hearing is impaired, it is almost impossible to shut it out. It can sometimes be a starting point for communication.

Not all musical experience is helpful. Some children quickly latch on to a particular music tape or video and need to hear it repeatedly. By offering a creative time with real live instruments you will be providing an environment which encourages spontaneity and relationship in a medium that the child already understands. Sharing music together can also give you the opportunity to praise her achievements which in turn might encourage her to want to try harder; not just to play music but to attract your attention generally.

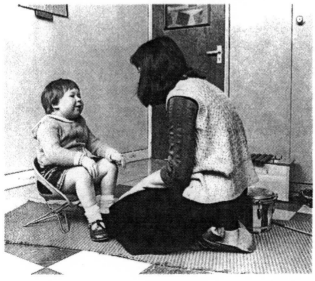

Part 2

How to Get Started

How Do I Begin?

By now you are probably saying to yourself, 'Yes, this sounds a good idea, but I'm not musical enough, I can't sing, I can't play an instrument and I certainly can't read music!'

First of all, none of the following suggestions will require you to learn a complicated instrument or to read music, and, most important of all, everybody is musical. You may have been told in the past that you sing out of tune or that you can't keep time. This is true for a very very small minority of people. However, if you start to think of musical enjoyment rather than performance, you will start to relax about the idea of playing music. Begin by thinking about your favourite song, CD or piece of music. If you can sing it to yourself or dance to it or tap your foot to it, it means you are musical. The first step in making music with your child is to understand that you are musical.

Here are some suggestions to help you feel more confident about singing and playing:

1. Try quietly humming to yourself.

2. If you listen to the radio, try singing along to the music you like when nobody is around.

3. Sing to yourself at some time during the day, for a week; you will be surprised how quickly your voice improves as you get used to using it.

4. Try dancing or clapping to music.

5. If you enjoy a particular piece of classical music, try humming along freely without words. Try Mozart or Bach for starters.

6. Listen to the same pieces or songs regularly. Get to know them and join in.

Helping your child through music making could be a long-term project so there is no point in rushing into it. Take as much time as you need to build up your confidence. You may want to make time to listen to some live music, go to a concert or get together with someone else who would like to use music with their child.

What Do I Need to Get Started?

You should aim towards building up a small collection of well-made instruments. It is better to be limited to a skin-head tambour than to have a lot of plastic drums and whistles which are cheap but sound uninteresting. The sound of the instruments is very important; the clearer the sound, the more it will help the child to focus her listening. Well-made instruments are expensive; however, they do last for a long time. It may be helpful for you to contact your national music therapy association, e.g. The Association of Professional Music Therapists, UK, The British Society for Music Therapy, The American Association of Music Therapy, The Australian Association of Music Therapy etc. Sometimes charitable funds are donated to these associations specifically for the purchase of instruments. Finding out where the nearest registered music therapist works will also be useful for you if you need any particular advice. Alternatively, your local portage worker, toy library or opportunity play group may be able to help.

The following list of instruments covers all the activities described in this booklet. Look through the activities and decide which of them is relevant to your child's developmental level.

from top right clockwise:
> *(i) a wooden xylophone with a pair of felt beaters (ii) A skin headed tambour with one rubber headed beater (iii)a pair of chinese cymbals (iv)a long african bean rattle (v) A pair of bongo drums without a stand (vi) two chime bars (one red one blue) with a pair of chime bar beaters (vii) a small seed rattle*

Basic instruments to collect over time

Skin tambour

Skin tambourine (covered with a head, not an open ring)

Chime bar C above middle C

Chime bar F below middle C (different colour from Chime bar C)

Felt beaters, two pairs, preferably with cork handles which can be enlarged by adding foam rubber

Chime bar beaters, hard, two pairs

African bean rattles, two different sounds

Reed horns, two (these come with a set of different pitch pipes included)

Wooden bongo drums

Wooden xylophone (not metal)

I would suggest you start by buying a tambour, a chime bar and some beaters.

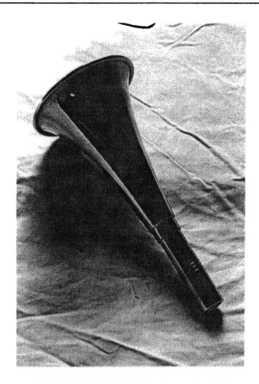

Most shops stock a wide range of educational instruments and will send a catalogue.

Rattles, cymbals and free-standing drums can sometimes be purchased more cheaply from ethnic shops or craft shops.

For further help with local suppliers contact:

British Society for Music Therapy
25 Rosslyn Avenue
East Barnet
Hertfordshire
EN4 8DH
Tel: 020 8368 8879

Planning Some Music Time

You probably know from experience that having a routine is important for the day-to-day care of your child. It is also important to define your music time as clearly as possible so that the child can anticipate making music. The following suggestions are to help you plan a music time lasting about 15 minutes at first.

1. Make music when your child is relatively alert, at the same time of the day, in the same room.

2. Make music in a place where you are not going to be disturbed by other children or the noise of television or radio. Remember, you are trying to focus your child's listening, so she will need as much silence around her music as possible.

3. Only use the instruments for your music time. Don't let the child play aimlessly with them or they will soon lose their interest and their connection with relationship through music.

4. Because you will be listening carefully to what the child is doing, try to keep music-making a one-to-one activity to begin with. Later on, when the child is

ready to share and take turns, you can involve other children, but always be sure that the child with special needs is setting the pace. Only involve other children if it is adding to the activity rather than detracting from it.

5. Plan which instruments you are going to use BEFORE you start and have a clear idea of what you are aiming at.

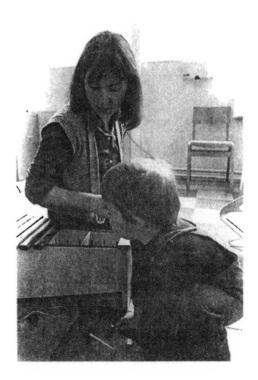

How to Play

There are a whole variety of ways you can use the simple percussion instruments listed. The following activities are merely guide-lines for your own playing. In the photographs you can see how different children have played the instruments and how we have developed games together. You may want to use the games as starting points for your playing. They are suggestions and may not work in exactly the same way as they did for the children in the illustrations. Try to develop a flexible approach to the instruments and adapt the following activities to suit the needs of your child.

Before you start, there are a few questions you should keep in mind as you go along:

- Is the child able to 'keep up' with you, or is your playing too fast or too slow?
- Is the child listening to what she is doing, or is she just banging away on the drum?
- Can the child hear both you and herself?
- Is the child repeating the same pattern over and over again, and losing herself in the activity?
- Is there enough space for 'questions' and 'answers' in the music?

- Have you matched your child's level of ability to the activity?

- Is the child using the instrument meaningfully, or has she reverted to sucking or chewing?

During music time you can afford to have high standards. After all, it is only 15 minutes or so, and 15 minutes concentrated effort from the child is worth guiding carefully.

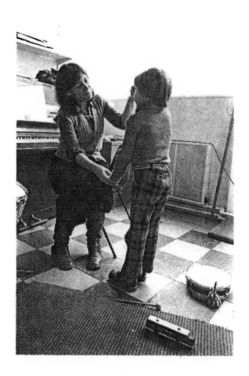

Part 3

Activities

The activities are labelled as very easy, easy, and more difficult, and are based around the use of different instruments. At first, choose instruments and activities which you think the child can manage, then later move on to more difficult ones.

The Drum

Exploring the Drum

It is a good idea to sit opposite the child, on the floor.

First, present the drum to her, so that the flat surface faces her.

Hold the drum whilst she explores it.

Wait and see what she does.

Show her that she can produce a sound by tapping it, once.

Resist the temptation to tap out one of your own patterns in the hope that she will imitate it. You must take your cues from her rather than lead the playing, so keep holding the drum and direct her hands towards it.

Wait and see what she does.

When she makes a strong tap, praise her in your usual way.

If she does not play you can hold her hand and let it drop onto the drum. As it hits the drum make a sound yourself to accentuate what the child has done, say 'Bang!' or 'Crash'.

Work towards repetition; if you find something attracts her attention – repeat it.

Be as free as you can with your own vocal sounds as she plays.

Let her show you what speed she wants to play at.

Really try hard not to beat with her hands on the drum. Wait for as long as it takes her to reach out and touch the surface of the drum – she may need more time to explore before she can play 'in time'.

The Tambourine

Up and Down Tambourine Game

This is a very simple sound conversation. The aim is to encourage imitation and create a dialogue.

Sitting opposite the child, get her attention by raising your hand to eye level whilst saying, 'UP'.

Hold your hand in the 'up' position for a moment.

As you say, 'DOWN' bring your hand down onto the tambourine.

Repeat 'UP' and 'DOWN'.

Present the drum to the child.

Get her attention and say 'UP' – wait for her to start raising her arm.

If she needs help do the action with her.

Hold the arm 'UP' for a second and then say 'DOWN' as she brings it down.

Try to make your voice go up and down as you play.

Repeat the sequence so that you are playing alternately.

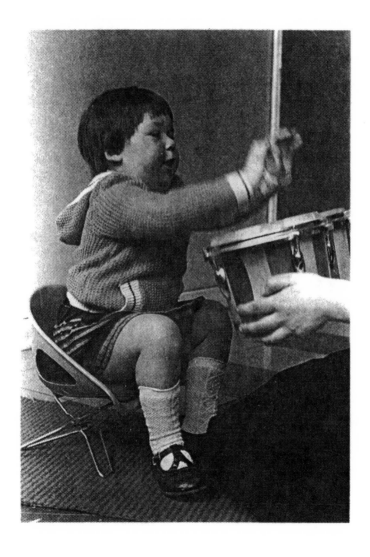

Holding a Beater

Holding and Using a Beater

At first it may be difficult to interest the child in using the beaters. However when she realises that she can make a more focused sound, she will start to use them more readily. For those children who throw objects, learning to hold and use, rather than hold and throw, can be an important step forward, so it is worth persevering. Use an activity which the child has already enjoyed or a song she already knows to invite her to hold a beater.

Position yourself with two beaters at the ready.

Offer the child a beater and let her explore it in her usual way.

After a short exploration begin your favourite beating game or song.

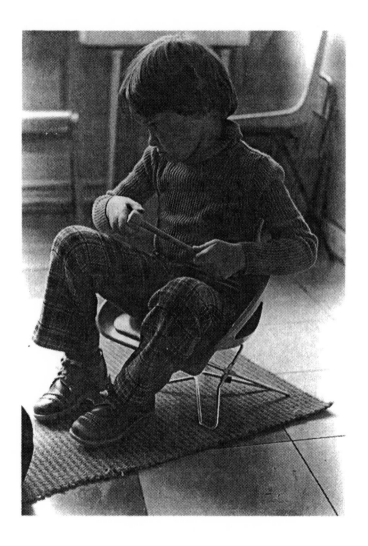

Try to avoid the beater being thrown or dropped because once this has happened it can appear more interesting to throw it than use it.

If necessary hold your hand firmly around the child's to support her grip. Placing foam rubber around the handle can help some children hold more easily.

Be careful to follow the speed of her beating.

Do not expect the child to enjoy using the beater the first time. If she is very resistive it may be enough simply to have the experience of making one tap.

Try not to lose patience and beat the drum for her; it is very important to listen to what the child is trying to do, however simple it may be. What you are aiming at is supporting and encouraging the child's attempts at playing rather than imposing musical patterns upon her. The child will very soon lose interest if she feels she cannot keep up.

Bongos

Using Bongo Drums

Bongos are useful as standing drums. Put them on the floor and they are a sturdy instrument with a good sound; hold them and they are light enough to be moved quickly towards the child.

Bongos are also useful for helping the child to make alternate hand movements. This in turn will help make her more aware of her two hands. In the case of cerebral-palsied children, or those with immature physical development, you can concentrate on getting the hands forward and down onto the drums simultaneously as this will help to increase balance and symmetrical muscle patterns.

Hold the drums so that the child does not have to reach down very far, just below chin level with the child. Tilt them towards her so that she can see what she is doing.

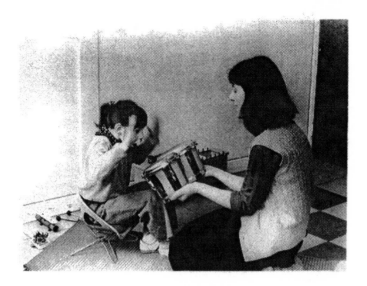

Let the child set the pace of the beating and sing to her as she beats.

Sing –   'Annie's beating on the BONG-GOS'
         'Annie's beating on the BONG-GOS'
         (*Or David's beating or Susie's beating –*
         according to the child's name).

Singing

Singing Songs to the Child's Drumming

When the child is able to sustain tapping at a regular pace, try extending the child's activity by singing to her as she plays. At first this may seem impossible, but once you have tried it you will find it is really not so difficult and will give the child a lot of stimulation. Get to know some simple tunes, possibly nursery rhymes or anything that you enjoy and can remember. Substitute new words for the words of the song. For example, instead of *Twinkle Twinkle, Little Star* sing – 'Dan is beating on the drum'. Make up your own words to describe what the child is doing, using the rhythm of the song. Choose two or three nursery rhymes to get to know because, however silly they may seem, children love them. *BaBa Black Sheep, Humpty Dumpty,* and *Jack and Jill* are quite adequate. If you are unsure how these songs sound, do borrow a tape or CD from a library. But whatever happens, try to avoid simply putting on the tape instead of singing the song yourself with your child. The reason being that you can adjust your speed and tempo to the specific speed of your child's drumming – a tape will just roll on over it. This is about allowing your child the opportunity to take responsibility for the timing of the music whilst you sing along with her.

Getting to Know a Song

Choose one song to get to know, either your own or a nursery rhyme.

Sing in time to the child's tapping.

When she knows the end of the song, try delaying the last line slightly so that she needs to listen to the words in order to know when to stop. This way, the child will have to listen to the sounds of the words and the length of the phrase.

Accenting the Phrase

Sing the song whilst holding the drum out of reach.

Bring the drum towards her as you finish the end of the line. Only let her tap on the last beat.

e.g.   'Jack and Jill went up the...hill
To fetch a pail of wa...ter
Jack fell down and broke his...crown
And Jill came tumbling af...ter.'

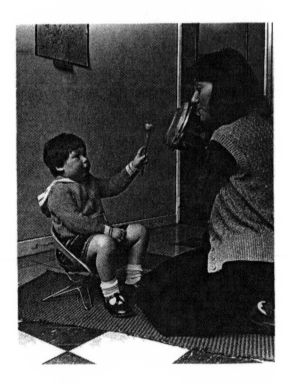

Rhythmic Names

Playing Names

Once the child can easily sustain drum beating and enjoys playing to your singing, you can invite her to imitate rhythmic patterns on the drum. This will help the child to distinguish the different sorts of rhythm in speech. Start by using the rhythm pattern of her name.

As usual, position yourself opposite the child.

Get her attention and tell her to 'Listen'.

Say and beat the rhythm of her name, slowly and clearly, but not so slowly that it loses the sound of the name.

<pre>
        !   !   !   !
e.g. Jen-ny or Je/mi-ma
</pre>

Repeat

Offer the drum to the child.

Even if she can't say her name she may, by now, be able to imitate the rhythmic drum sound of her name.

If she uses the drum to start beating repeatedly, stop her by removing the drum.

You may need to repeat the pattern again and again, but always leave time and space for the child to attempt the imitation each time you play it. Somehow you have got to make it clear that this is a new game.

If she still persists in free beating, try to remove the drum after the correct number of beats. This way you will be showing her, through the sound she is producing, that you want her to play a short pattern.

When the child achieves her drum name, try to resist getting her to *say* her name as well.

Praise her and repeat the game.

When you feel that she is secure in what she is doing introduce another name with the same rhythmic pattern

　　!　　!

e.g. Da-ddy.

Later on, you can move on to another pattern altogether, but don't rush. The important thing to remember is that music should be fun. If the child senses you pushing her on too quickly she may withdraw.

Chime Bars

Using the Chime Bars

Playing the chime bar demands more control from the child, so don't start using them until she has gained some control of holding a beater. If you are having difficulty in getting her to hold a beater, the chime bar may interest her more than the drum. At whatever stage you introduce the chime bars, you should always aim to produce a good clear sound which the child can enjoy listening to. There is not much point in using the chimes as you would a drum and beating in time with them. It is much more effective to use them 'melodically' rather than 'rhythmically'.

Single Sounds

Place a beater next to the child and ask her to pick it up.

Even if you don't think she will respond to this request, eventually she may, as she learns that to play the chime bar you *need* a beater.

As an introduction to the chime bar sound spend some time playing alternate individual notes, slowly and clearly. First you, then the child, you, then the child, and so on.

Then use the other chime bar and explore its sound in the same way.

As the child gets better at playing accurately, move the bars further away, so that she has to stretch out to find them.

You can use this play to emphasise the careful use of the beaters.

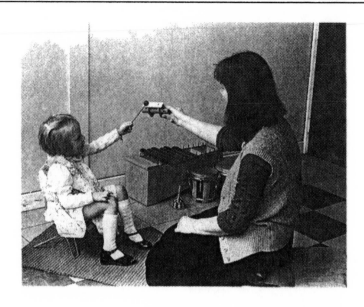

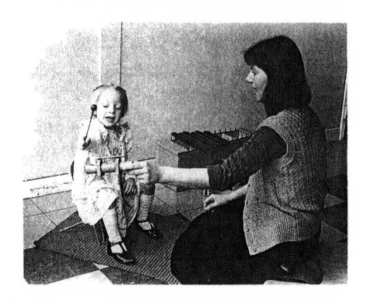

MORE DIFFICULT

Two Note Playing with Colours

When you get the chime bars try to buy different coloured ones as this will help the child to identify the difference in sound, and the difference in sound will in turn help to identify the difference in colour.

A very simple game can be played with your two chime bars.

One is 'High' and the other is 'Low'. (Make sure you can hear the difference!)

Ask the child to pick up the beater you have placed at her side.

Hold one bar in each hand and move them in rotation.

Sing: !   !

> 'The high one and the low one,
> The high one and the low one,
> The high one and the low one,
> David can play'.

Make up your own simple tune and substitute the correct name.

Try putting the bars high up and then low down
as you sing 'High' and 'Low'.

Play the game again this time singing:

!   !

'The red one and the blue one,
  It's the red one and the blue one,
  The red one and the blue one,
  David can play'.

Make sure the child plays the appropriate colour
as you sing it.

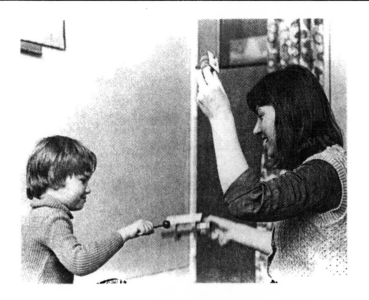

EASY

Playing Chime Bars with Songs or Other Instruments

You can use the chime bars while singing songs, but use them sparingly.

Offer one to the child to emphasise the end of a phrase rather than as a continuous background to the singing. This way the child is more likely to make her own vocal sounds as she anticipates the shape of the phrases.

                                                   !

e.g. 'BaBa Black sheep, have you any wool?

                            !

    Yes Sir, Yes Sir, three bags full.

                                     !

    One for the Master and one for the Dame...'
and so forth

You can combine the chime bars with other instruments to form a small group of sounds.

For example, make sound patterns for the child to imitate, using chime bars, bongo drums and a tambour:

- Two beats on the bongos, followed by one beat on a chime bar
- One beat on the high chime bar, followed by one beat on the tambour and finished by one beat on the low chime bar

Play the patterns slowly and clearly, and listen out for any attempts the child may make to give you patterns to imitate. Remember, you are always aiming at 'conversations'.

Rattles

Using Rattles

There are many different types of rattles available. You will need to think carefully about your child's ability to hold and use the object when choosing an appropriate rattle. There are different types of rattles which are available from shops that specialise in ethnic goods.

The first one shown is a long string rattle made of large beans. This type of rattle can be used to swing to and fro between you and the child, to shake up and down or explore in detail. As you can see, Jemima is working hard at catching and shaking as I sing to her in time with the swinging instrument.

The more usual type of rattle is also shown – a small hand-held instrument. Let the child explore the rattle first and then help her to use it rhythmically. You can also use it on the drum head to get a louder sound. It is important to use these instruments sparingly. Otherwise, the listening experience is dulled and the sound becomes too familiar to be of much interest to the child.

Rattle sounds go nicely with drum sounds, so play freely and try to improvise a song as you go, then exchange instruments.

Clapping

Clapping Music

It seems obvious to mention clapping as a musical activity, but it is something which can be overlooked because it is so simple. For some children clapping to music is one of the few organised activities they find stimulating and it is very helpful to go back yourself to that most simple of musical activities and join with the child in clapping to a song.

You can see that Kelly's interest is held and sustained by our clapping game. We have extended our claps to become exaggerated movements which she finds funny and exciting.

Explore your child's interest in clapping and touching in time. The most important thing to remember in this game is that the shared play you are both engaged in can be extended by either of you, so watch carefully what the child does.

Imitate her as she imitates you, and enjoy the play as she enjoys it. Use simple songs that she knows, or make up your own clapping song:

e.g.   'Clapping, clapping, clapping, clapping,
Clapping to the Mu-sic.
Kelly's clapping, clapping, clapping,
Clapping to the Mu-sic.'

Small Cymbals

Using Chinese Hand Cymbals

Inexpensive, and attractive to the child, these hand cymbals can be used with children with severe disabilities. If the child cannot hold them individually you can suspend them so that the child can feel them and brush them together to make a sound.

Here, Kelly has explored the cymbals, turned them around and succeeded in using them on her own. I am playing a drum in time with her playing as I sing a simple tune to support and encourage her music.

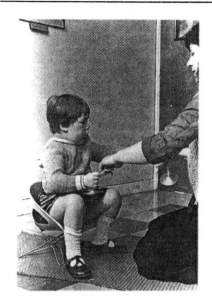

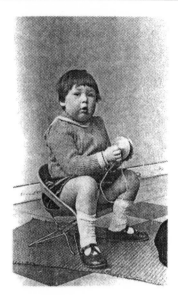

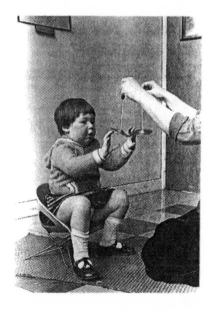

Horns

Using Horns

The reed horns you can see in the photograph are good for encouraging closure of the lips and for making the child generally more aware of changes in mouth position. This in turn can help her towards forming mouth positions for words. Blowing is also a helpful experience in learning to make words.

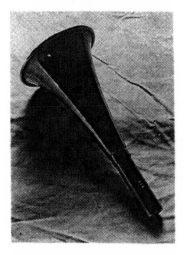

[A note about hygiene: when using blowing instruments it is important to have some wipes available in case of transferring infection. You will probably be using these anyway to deal with coughs, sneezes or dribbling on other instruments and particularly with beaters which tend to get sucked or chewed from time to time.]

Getting to Know the Horn

Position yourself comfortably opposite the child.

Show her the horn and then pick it up and blow it slowly and clearly.

Offer the horn to the child.

Let her explore it and then help her to hold it appropriately.

The child may not want to put the horn in her mouth, so let her hold it whilst you blow it again.

It may take some time before the child will try to blow, so don't force her to put it in her mouth.

Even if she can't make a sound, praise her for her attempts and repeat the horn sound yourself.

Offer her the horn again.

Horn Song

Choose a song you both know and substitute the word at the end of each line with a horn tone.

Keep hold of the horn and offer it to the child at the right moment.

Let her blow it and then gently remove it as you sing the beginning of the next line.

Although she may not be able to sing the words of the song, the child will be directly concentrating on the phrase length and the position of the word in the phrase:

e.g.   'Polly put the kettle–*horn tone!*
Polly put the kettle–*horn tone!*
Polly put the kettle–*horn tone!*
We'll all have–*horn tone!*' and so forth…

As she gets to know this game, work towards getting the child to keep hold of the horn so that eventually she controls the horn tones herself.

Xylophone

Using the Xylophone

The wooden xylophone shown here is an ideal instrument for concentrated playing. It offers many opportunities for imitation and motor control – control both of movements and of timing. It is, however, the most expensive of the instruments I have discussed. I include it here because you may have the opportunity of influencing a playgroup budget, or of buying one together with some other parents.

Suggestions for Your Own Playing

The good thing about the xylophone is that you can choose a 'scale'. Try putting these different series of notes on the frame:

C D E G A C D E G A	E F# A C E F# A C D
C D E F G A B C	A B D E G A D E
D E F G A D E F G A	G A C E F F# G A
C D F# G C D F# G	B♭ C D E F# B♭ C D E F

The xylophone can be used very freely once you have gained some confidence in your own ideas.

You may need to practice playing in time by clapping or using a hand drum.

Then move onto the xylophone, playing up and down the scale you have chosen. Don't try to make complicated tunes, just play each note evenly up and down the scale in time to your counting. Once you can do this, you can begin to be a bit more adventurous by leaping notes and thus making melodies.

Practice playing to the following counts. (The stress marks above the numbers indicate that you should emphasise the note).

123 123 123 123

123456   123456   123456

12312   12312   12312

1234 1234   1234   1234   1234

12345678 12345678

12 12 12 12 12

Xylophone Games

As you can see from the picture opposite, you can hold the xylophone on your lap so that it tilts towards the child. This reduces the possibility of the pieces springing off. Make sure also that the pieces are pegged from your side of the frame.

Don't worry about playing songs or tunes that you know on the xylophone. You can use it much more freely by making up your own sung melodies over the top of the scale you are using. Practice singing to your own playing.

It will be too much to expect the child to learn to play her own favourite tune on the instrument. What you are aiming for is imitation of WAYS of playing, rather than learning exact tunes.

Up and down playing (hard rubber beaters)

This game is really the same as the up and down drum game, although it demands more concentration from the child.

Position yourself comfortably opposite one another.

Get the child's attention by saying, 'Watch!'

Make a very large movement upwards with your arm.

Hold it for a moment and bring your beater down onto one of the tones.

Tell the child it is her turn.

Help her, if necessary, to make her own tone, anywhere on the xylophone.

Repeat, until a nice flow of tones is being played; first you, then the child, and so on.

As you can see, the child will be watching what you are doing and listening carefully to what is happening.

Glissando game

In contrast to the careful up and down movements you have been making, now show the child a very clear run across the tones, producing a harp-like sound. Start from the child's easiest position, so that if she is right-handed start from your left and draw the beater all the way across the tones in one movement.

Repeat and then let her try to imitate how you have played.

Play alternate glissandi, first you, then the child, until you are playing in time with one another. Then improvise a simple melodic line with your voice. You don't have to use words, just 'La La' softly with the sounds you are making, in time with your movements. You may be surprised to hear her join in with the singing.

MORE DIFFICULT

Contrasting playing

After the child has learned these two different ways of playing, play together but keep changing your playing from glissandi to up and down tones. Give the child enough time at each sound to feel confident before you change it. The child may imitate your changes in playing so then see if you can imitate her changes in playing by letting her play how she likes and listening to what she does.

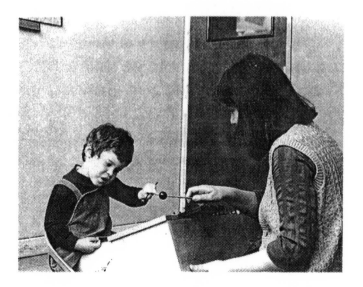

MORE DIFFICULT

Divide the Xylophone

When the child has gained some control at playing, divide the tones so that you have two, and the child has five or six. You are aiming to increase her control by limiting where she can play on the frame.

Leave a gap between your notes and hers, so that yours are at one end and hers are at the other.

Tell her that she can only play her tones and must not play yours.

Play your tones together and then switch around so that the child has only two tones to concentrate on. Occasionally you must cheat and play her tones instead of your own, then it will be more exciting and she will start to cheat as well. This will demand a lot of concentration, as good games always do.

Movement

Walking to Music

As I discussed earlier, music invites movement, and for those children who are still unsteady walkers, or who need to be helped to balance, music may help them to organise their movements more accurately. The main thing to remember about walking to music is that the music must be at the child's pace. It is no good putting on a tape and expecting the child to be able to move in time.

Unless you are sure that a certain piece of music goes at the speed of the child, use your own singing and drumming. You are infinitely more flexible than recorded music and you can stop and start with the child or slow down, if necessary. Here Claire and I are walking carefully together, and I am singing a walking song as we go. Later on she moves on her own to the music.

Conclusion

By connecting with your child through music you are offering a chance to increase communication and decrease isolation. The activities in this book will not work in the same way for each and every child. Each child is an individual; the beauty of music making is that it can meet each unique child in an individual way. Finding the confidence to develop your own ideas may take time, but the principles I have discussed can be adapted to any musical improvisations or songs you decide to try out. Perhaps the most important thing to focus on is tuning in to the pace at which your child responds, being able to wait for her response and discovering, together, the speed of the music.

Working on this revised edition of 'Making Music with the Young Child with Special Needs' I am taken back into the room where these photographs were first taken, more than twenty years ago at Charing Cross Hospital in London. The children featured here will now be mature young adults out in the world; whether they have professional careers, work in a sheltered environment or are being cared for at home. Some of them will have children of their own by now. I am grateful to each one of them for having taught me so much in my early career as a music therapist. Their musical journeys have been an inspiration to many parents and children over the years and their obvious delight in making music remains an inspiration.

Music therapy has also come a long way since this book was first published. It is now a state registered profession in the UK. Should you wish to find out where music therapy is available to you through the NHS or through your Education Services, you can contact the Council for Professions Supplementary to Medicine or the Association of Professional Music Therapists, UK, who will help put you in touch with your regional branch of the APMT and the registered music therapists who are working in your area.

For readers abroad there are now national music therapy associations in most countries. If you need help in finding them the Association of Professional Music Therapists, UK may be able to help.

Good luck with your music making. I hope very much that you enjoy it.

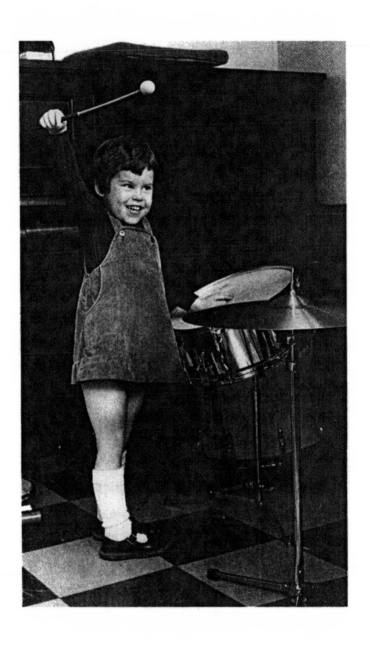

The Author

Elaine Streeter trained as a music therapist in 1974 with Paul Nordoff and Clive Robbins. She went on to train as a teacher in special education and was then appointed by the ILEA to work as a music therapist and special educator with young children at the Child Development Centre Charing Cross Hospital. In 1977 she completed a post-graduate music degree at the University of York with the first university-based research dissertation on music therapy in the UK. In 1981 she was appointed Senior Lecturer in Music Therapy at the Roehampton Institute of Higher Education with the brief to develop a new post-graduate training course for music therapists. In 1989 she completed a three-year training course in psychodynamic counselling at the Westminster Pastoral Foundation.

For the last ten years she has been involved in supervising and training music therapists as well as working with adult clients and children with special needs. She is a visiting professor at the

Guildhall School of Music and Drama in London and also lectures at Anglia Polytechnic University, Cambridge. She is an approved supervisor for the Association of Professional Music Therapists, UK and is well known internationally as a specialist in her field.

Index

Easy for the Child, More Difficult for You

More Difficult

Printed in the United Kingdom by
Lightning Source UK Ltd., Milton Keynes
139155UK00001B/9/A

9 781853 029608